MW00943138

Revival's Secret

The Compelling Reason
We Really Do Not Want Revival

PAUL
SCHWANKE

First published by Paul Schwanke, an Independent Baptist
evangelist from Lakeside Baptist Church of Peoria, Arizona.
Evangelist Schwanke is committed to preaching
and providing materials to assist pastors and churches
in the fulfillment of the Great Commission.

Evangelist Paul Schwanke
www.preachthebible.com

Cover design by Mr. Rick Lopez
Special thanks to Pastor Ken Brooks

ISBN-13: 978-1497461864
ISBN-10: 1497461863

Printed in the United States of America

CONTENTS

IT WAS NOT the "best of times; the worst of times." It was simply the worst of times.

The days were incredibly evil. Pick your Hitler, your Pol Pot, your Idi Amin, and they would have nothing on King Manasseh. He ascended the throne of Judah at the age of twelve as a rebel bent on undoing the righteous reforms of his father. The indictments recorded in the Bible against him are numerous: he practiced the abominations of the pagans; he rebuilt the houses of false religion and idolatry; he worshipped the sun and the stars; he brazenly desecrated the house of God.

The Bible describes him with these despicable words: "Manasseh seduced them to do more evil than did the nations whom the LORD destroyed before the children of Israel" (2 Kings 21:9). To make matters worse, he wasn't voted out of office after eight years. He ruled Jerusalem and Judah for 55 miserable, disgraceful years, ultimately provoking God to say, "Behold, I *am* bringing *such* evil upon Jerusalem and Judah, that whosoever heareth of it, both his ears shall tingle...I will wipe Jerusalem as *a man* wipeth a dish, wiping *it*, and turning *it* upside down" (2 Kings 21:12-13).

Manasseh was famous for his wickedness, but one particularly abhorrent act has remained as a testimony to this vile man. Desiring to pacify his pagan idol, he offered his own children on a fiery altar, callously murdering his own sons. Sixty years later, Jeremiah reminded the people that God had not forgotten (Jeremiah 7:31-34).

Manasseh was so nefarious and opprobrious, he literally plunged to the moral basement reserved for an abortion doctor. "Manasseh shed innocent blood very much, till he had filled Jerusalem from one end to another" (2 Kings 21:16). This bloody king was not satisfied with the slaughter of his own offspring; he practiced genocide in the name of his religion.

Cushi and his wife must have been terrorized.

Holding her newborn son, Mrs. Cushi could only fear the worst. Her nation promoted infanticide and this precious child with royal blood flowing through his little veins would make an ideal offering to this satanic cult. Her son was the grandson of Gedaliah, the great grandson of Amariah, and the great, great grandson of the last righteous king, Hezekiah. A sacrifice of a descendant of such a king would be a prize indeed.

It would not be hard to imagine Cushi attempting to comfort her. "Remember the story of Amram and Jochebed? There was no hope for a boy born in Egypt yet God gave them a way. They made an ark of the bulrushes and God hid little Moses in the Nile River! Remember Elijah? God found a way to hide him from King Ahab!

"If God can hide Moses and Elijah then we will just trust him to hide our baby. In fact that would make a great name! We will call him 'hidden of God!'

"We will call him - Zephaniah!"

Chapter One

The Product of Revival Preaching

IT WAS THE PROPHET Micah who preached this glorious message of hope:

"Who *is* a God like unto thee, that pardoneth iniquity, and passeth by the transgression of the remnant of his heritage? he retaineth not his anger for ever, because he delighteth *in* mercy. He will turn again, he will have compassion upon us; he will subdue our iniquities; and thou wilt cast all their sins into the depths of the sea. Thou wilt perform the truth to Jacob, *and* the mercy to Abraham, which thou hast sworn unto our fathers from the days of old" (Micah 7:18-20).

It was the last message Judah would hear from Heaven for seven decades. The sins of Manasseh infected his country, but those sins, as heinous as they were, were not the biggest problem. Their greatest need was to hear from God, yet with the wickedness filling the land, God was not playing their game. Heaven was silent. There was no message.

As the 2012 presidential election was being played out in America, the religious polling firm, the Barna Group, surveyed born again Americans to discern their greatest concerns for America and their motivation for voting. To the evangelical voter, the candidates' positions on the following issues most influenced their vote:

Taxes 76%; Abortion 71%; Terrorism 71%; Immigration 67%; Gay Marriage 63%[1]

Presumably if we asked the saved citizens of America to describe the greatest issues of America, the list would resemble their response to the Barna Group. But if we could ask the prophet Amos the same question he would respond like this:

"Behold, the days come, saith the Lord GOD, that I will send a famine in the land, not a famine of bread, nor a thirst for water, but of hearing the words of the LORD: And they shall wander from sea to sea, and from the north even to the east, they shall run to and fro to seek the word of the LORD, and shall not find it" (Amos 8:11-12).

Certainly we have enough Bibles in America. 88% of American adults own a Bible. 80% believe the Bible is sacred. The families that have Bibles have an average of 4.4 of them. 77% believe that American morals are sliding and they say that the overwhelming reason for the moral slippage is the lack of the Bible in our country.[2]

Though we seem to have a healthy respect for the Bible, there remains a difference between owning a Bible and submitting to it. In the same survey, only 21% of the respondents actually read the Bible at least four times a week! We have Bibles but we get no message from them.

The scenario is repeated in compromising churches across the land. 40,000 people fill an auditorium in Houston every week where they are joined by millions in more than 100 countries around the world. They watch Joel Osteen hold a Bible in the air and say:

"This is my Bible. I am what it says I am. I can do what it says I can do. Today, I will be taught the Word of God."

He proceeds with a message of human psychology mixed with tiny amounts of Scripture. Verses warning of Hell and judgment are always avoided. People are convinced they have heard from the Word of God but they have not. He personifies the great problem in our land - we think we have the Bible but we do not.

Imagine seventy years passing without a verse of the Bible. Seventy years without a message convicting us of our sins. Seventy years without God's leadership and direction. The last time God spoke to Jerusalem He told them He delighted in mercy, yet they had spent seventy years spurning that mercy. Seven decades of silence are about to come to an end as Zephaniah steps to the pulpit to preach.

We can almost hear the compromising priests and prophets welcome the man of God with these words: "Zephaniah, what word of comfort do you have for us? What pleasing words from Heaven will soothe us today? Zephaniah, won't you share what the Lord has laid on your heart?"

So the man of God opens his mouth, and for the first time since the days of Micah they hear from God:

"I will utterly consume all *things* from off the land, saith the LORD" (Zephaniah 1:2).

Nothing like warming up the crowd! It is probably safe to say that Joel Osteen will not be preaching that verse. It would be easy to imagine the ministerial association of Zephaniah's day choking on those words. Most likely, they had never heard such preaching in their entire lives, and as they were cleaning the wax out of their ears, the man of God pressed the pedal to the floor:

"I will consume man and beast; I will consume the fowls of the heaven, and the fishes of the sea, and the stumblingblocks with the wicked; and I will cut off man from off the land, saith the LORD. I will also stretch out mine hand upon Judah, and upon all the inhabitants of Jerusalem; and I will cut off the remnant of Baal from this place, *and* the name of the Chemarims with the priests; And them that worship the host of heaven upon the housetops; and them that worship *and* that swear by the LORD, and that swear by Malcham; And them that are turned back from the LORD; and *those* that have not sought the LORD, nor enquired for him" (Zephaniah 1:3-6).

That would just about cover everybody.

What would happen in America if every man of God preached such a message of judgment on Sunday morning? What if, instead of sharing what we have on our hearts, we actually opened the Bible and preached like the men of God did? What if we actually warned people about the judgment of God?

What would happen if we had a generation of preachers that were like the preachers in the Bible? What if we preached like Elijah and Elisha and Jeremiah and Ezekiel and Isaiah and Jonah and Amos and Zechariah and John the Baptist and Stephen and Paul? What would happen if, just for one Sunday, pulpits had men that determined to "Cry aloud, spare not, lift up thy voice like a trumpet, and shew my people their transgression, and the house of Jacob their sins" (Isaiah 58:1)?

What if, just for a brief moment, we actually stepped in the pulpit proclaiming: "But truly I am full of power by the spirit of the LORD, and of judgment, and of might, to declare unto Jacob his transgression, and to Israel his sin" (Micah 3:8). What if a minister went home next Sunday saying: "I have preached righteousness in the great congregation: lo, I have not refrained my lips, O LORD, thou knowest" (Psalm 40:9). What if next Sunday at high noon, people walked out of an auditorium knowing "that there hath been a prophet among them" (Ezekiel 2:5).

What might happen, if just for one Sunday morning, a pastor would not worry about the tax exempt status of his church but would publicly call out the name of an adulterous politician and exclaim, "It is not lawful for thee to have her" (Matthew 14:4). What if a man of God would condemn the compromising seminary professors paid by convention salaries and charge: "Ye stiffnecked and uncircumcised in heart and ears, ye do always resist the Holy Ghost: as your fathers *did*, so *do* ye" (Acts 7:51).

Suppose for a moment men of God had the courage to preach against the purveyors of false religion and conclude the message with "*Ye* serpents, *ye* generation of vipers, how can ye escape the damnation of hell" (Matthew 23:33).

What would happen if men with the courage of Zephaniah stepped into the pulpits without fear and favor to thunder the word of God?

We just might produce a Josiah.

Chapter Two
Revival Preaching and Time

JOSIAH'S STORY is the story of revival. When his evil grandfather, Manasseh, died after 55 years of disastrous leadership, the father of Josiah, Amon, ascended the throne of Judah. It did not take long to realize there was no desire to change course, for Amon "did *that which was* evil in the sight of the LORD, as did Manasseh his father...(he) humbled not himself before the LORD...but Amon trespassed more and more" (2 Chronicles 33:22-23). The servants of Amon could stand it no longer, so they assassinated him and crowned an eight year old boy as king. From 640-609 BC, Josiah led the land down the road of revival, an awakening, it would turn out, that would be Judah's last gasp before the wrath of God cascaded upon the land.

We often look at historical revivals as a moment in time. We hear the story of God moving in unusual ways and pinpoint them to a certain incident, but a true moving of God always has the 'rest of the story'. There may be a sickly, frail woman who bombards the throne of God hour after hour. Perhaps men meet early in the morning to seek God and plead for His working. The great manifestations of the power of God always have an unseen catalyst that will never be known until the Judgment Seat of Christ.

On September 23, 1857, Evangelist Jeremiah Lanphier started a noontime prayer meeting hoping businessmen would come during their lunch hour and pray for revival. Only one man came. They prayed together then agreed to meet the second week. Gradually the crowd grew, and that prayer meeting ultimately instigated the Third Great Awakening where close to one million people were saved.[3]

In the spring of 1904, a young Welshman named Evan Roberts was repeatedly awakened to pray from 1:00 to 5:00 a.m. Eleven years of praying brought a powerful, spiritual awakening to Wales.[4] Revival came to north China in 1932 in answer to several years of prayer of a Norwegian missionary, Maria Monsen.[5]

Revivals do not happen in a night. It can take months, even years of work before the ground is prepared and the seed is planted. 'Barking revivals' are a dime a dozen, but a mighty work from Heaven never comes cheaply. Somebody has to work a long time and pay a great price.

The revival under Josiah was not an instantaneous incident that landed on his lap. There were a series of important decisions that he made in his personal life over the course of a decade that ultimately opened Heaven's spigot.

Josiah was eight years old when he became king. At the age of 16 he made his first great decision when he "began to seek after the God of David his father" (2 Chronicles 34:3). Four years later at age 20, he chose to "purge Judah and Jerusalem" by ridding the land of the idols, altars, and evil worship centers. He was so intense in his hatred of false religion that he opened the tombs of pagan priests and burned their bones on altars. Later, he took his campaign to clean up the religious mess of Israel to the distant city of Bethel and in so doing fulfilled a prophecy given 300 years earlier:

"And, behold, there came a man of God out of Judah by the word of the LORD unto Bethel: and Jeroboam stood by the altar to burn incense. And he cried against the altar in the word of the LORD, and said, O altar, altar, thus saith the LORD; Behold, a child shall be born unto the house of David, Josiah by name; and upon thee shall he offer the priests of the high places that burn incense upon thee, and men's bones shall be burnt upon thee" (1 Kings 13:1-2).

At age 26 he determined to repair the long neglected house of God. The money was raised, the timber and stone was purchased, the carpenters, builders, and masons were hired, and the project commenced. In the course of the work, the high priest Hilkiah found the Bible. Perhaps Manasseh attempted to wipe the law of God out, yet Satan has always lost that fight. God miraculously protected and preserved His word until it was discovered by a faithful man.

Hilkiah gave the Scriptures to the Secretary of State (the scribe) Shaphan, who in turn read the Word of God to King Josiah. When he heard the message of the impending wrath of God upon his land, he was smitten, immediately humbled himself, and ripped his clothes. Messengers were sent to the prophetess Huldah who told Josiah that God indeed would judge the idolatry of the land, but he would be spared for his tender heart.

The king responded by gathering the elders of the land at the temple. The people of the capital city Jerusalem and the entire nation of Judah were present, both small and great, to listen to the reading of the Word of God. Josiah proceeded to make a covenant with God, promising that the nation would "walk after the LORD, and...keep his commandments and his testimonies and his statutes with all *their* heart and all *their* soul...(and) perform the words of this covenant that were written in this book" (2 Kings 23:4). The people stood with Josiah in agreement.

In 2 Kings 23:4-24 the record gives an impressive list of 21 different actions Josiah took to clean up Jerusalem and all the land of Judah. He was a holy terror indeed, raining judgment upon the false idols of Baal and those who brought the sin into the land. With powerful passion he tried to undo the sins of his grandfather, and for good measure, he fixed messes that went all the way back to Solomon. It was so impressive, God commented like this:

"And like unto him was there no king before him, that turned to the LORD with all his heart, and with all his soul, and with all his might, according to all the law of Moses; neither after him arose there *any* like him" (2 Kings 23:25).

That, my friend, is revival!

It begs the question: who influenced Josiah? Who was used of God to ignite such a flame in the depths of his soul? Who taught him to hate false religion and its corresponding idols? Who burned in his young bones a love and respect for the Word of God? Who instilled a hatred for the murderous sins of Manasseh and the filthy fornication of the religious harlots and sodomites? Who convinced him that centuries of Satanic religion could not only be combated, but that battle could be won?

Obviously, Josiah did not get his convictions from his father or his grandfather. He did not get the principles from the false ministers of Baal nor from the weak prophets and priests of Jehovah who lacked the backbone to stand against the tide of compromise.

When the commentators try to answer the question, they invariably make a guess that sounds like this: "Evidently he had spiritually motivated advisers or regents."[6]

Nice try, but we don't need to guess. The Bible tells us:

"The word of the LORD which came unto Zephaniah...in the days of Josiah the son of Amon, king of Judah" (Zephaniah 1:1).

A young king was listening.

Chapter Three
The Missing Element

ASK THE AVERAGE CHRISTIAN for the recipe of revival and invariably you will hear him say, "If my people, which are called by my name, shall humble themselves, and pray, and seek my face, and turn from their wicked ways; then will I hear from heaven, and will forgive their sin, and will heal their land" (2 Chronicles 7:14). But what does God use to bring people to such a place? How does God soften hearts and enable such contrition?

The revivals we read about in the Bible were fires ignited by preaching. The revival on Mount Carmel was a response to the convicting message of Elijah. When revival visited Nineveh there was the prophet Jonah preaching a simple but pointed message. Ezra, Nehemiah, and the Apostles in the book of Acts similarly demonstrate the importance of preaching in relation to revival.

The book of Zephaniah is the most comprehensive book of the Bible dealing with revival preaching. The impressive choices of Josiah that altered the course of his nation were fueled by some notable messages and a notable messenger. When the Bible is correctly preached, in content and in style, there will be consequences. The preaching will make them 'glad', or it will make them 'mad', but there will be a response.

We have witnessed Satan's assault against preaching. Hollywood and its cohorts in the news media deride all preachers as Bible thumping idiots. Even the word 'preaching' has a negative connotation to it, as the last thing self-centered humans want is someone 'preaching' to them. As such, seminary classrooms are producing ministerial students who are trained to give people what they want, which is someone that will soothe them and tell them how good they are.

What they need is someone who will "preach the word" (2 Timothy 4:2).

Look at the ice cream and cookies diet that religious people are feasting on a weekly basis. Use the remote control on a Sunday morning, and the religious channels are full of liars preaching a prosperity gospel. God does not want us rich or healthy or successful. He wants us to be saved from Hell.

Look at the religious 'talk shows'. Instead of a man of God condemning the world and its way, people want a spiritual alternative to Oprah. They want religious psychobabble which produces in the religious world the same result it does in the secular world - people who are convinced to ignore the guilt of their own sins.

Look at the auditoriums people fill on a Sunday morning. Instead of a well-lit building conducive for people reading their Bibles and learning the Word of God, they walk into a dimly lit theatre telling them to expect entertainment. The lights are on the entertainers, not the Bible.

Look at their ministers. Instead of a man appropriately dressed as an ambassador for the King of Kings, many look like their golf game has been interrupted. Instead of a respectful title due a man who is to be esteemed "very highly" (1 Thessalonians 5:13), people are taught to address their pastor like a neighbor over the fence.

Add to it a music program right out of our pagan culture, a program full of Hollywood glitz and glamor, put a Starbucks in the lobby, and it would be pretty hard to see any scenario where people are going to fear God. And when there "is no fear of God before their eyes" (Romans 3:18), we are as far from revival as we can humanly be.

How can we expect people to fear God when preachers will not preach about the fear of God? How will people tremble before the living God of the Bible when the minister displays a shallow, casual attitude with the message entrusted to Him? How can we expect God's people to have a passion for God when their pastor does not have a passion for the Bible?

A young Teddy Roosevelt living in New York City had a terrorizing fear of the Madison Square Church. He refused to set a foot inside the building if he were alone. His mother, Mittie, discovered her boy was afraid of something called 'zeal'. He was certain that 'zeal' was crouched in the dark corners of the church ready to jump at him. When she asked what a 'zeal' might be, he said he was not sure, but thought it was probably a large animal like an alligator or a dragon. He heard the minister read about it from the Bible. Using a concordance, she read him those passages containing the word zeal until he told her to stop. The line was from John 2:17: "And his disciples remembered that it was written, The zeal of thine house hath eaten me up."[7]

The future president didn't know how accurate he was! When zeal filled the heart of Jesus in the temple, He was a living terror. He "made a scourge of small cords, he drove them all out of the temple, and the sheep, and the oxen... (he) poured out the changers' money, and overthrew the tables" (John 2:15). When He was done, they didn't know what to think of Him, but they feared Him.

When the fear of God fell upon Josiah, it was the result of the preaching of Zephaniah. If the fear of God will return today, it will be fired by the impassioned preaching of a man of God proclaiming the Word of God. There is no 'plan B.'

And a young king was listening.

Chapter Four

Revival Preaching And Judgment

IMAGINE 57 YEARS without the Bible. As this book is written, 2013 is turning into 2014. What if America had not seen a Bible since 1957? What if the last Bible message anyone could recall was preached during the Eisenhower administration, when America was a nation of 48 states? What if 275 million people under the age of 60 in the United States had never once in their life heard a man of God hold the Bible and preach?

It was the scenario in Zephaniah 1. After decades of heavenly silence the prophet of God was instructed to declare a message from God. What would he say? What would you say? More importantly, what did God want him to say?

Revival preaching starts with "the word of the LORD" (Zephaniah 1:1). In the Old Testament that simple phrase delineates the man of God as a messenger of God. The five words inform the hearer that the prophet is not dispensing his opinion or advice, he is declaring the very words from the mouth of God. Of the 242 occurrences of this phrase, 225 of them describe the very method that God's man received God's word.[8]

As Jesus put it, "Man shall not live by bread alone, but by every word that proceedeth out of the mouth of God" (Matthew 4:4). That single verse pretty much settles the inspiration debate, doesn't it?

Zephaniah has a job to do. One doesn't have to read very far before the man of God is describing the wrath of God about to fall upon the land. For nearly 60 years, miserable seeds of perverseness had been planted in the land and it was harvest time. The revival preaching of Zephaniah taught powerful lessons about the judgment of God.

God's judgment is personal. There were nine occasions in Zephaniah chapter one where the preacher quotes Almighty God using the phrase "I will." God did not say, "I might; I could; I should." He said, "I will."

The pronouncements from Heaven are reinforced with the phrase "saith the Lord," a statement found six times through the book of Zephaniah. Every time the man of God cries those words, the hammer of judgment pounds the nail of guilt a little deeper. God is doing the judging. "This is what He said, and this is what He told me to say to you."

Religion today refuses a God of such judgment. Soft Christians have been conditioned to think that "God never does anything to us; He only does things for us." Yet that philosophy, which cannot be defended from the Bible, is contradicted repeatedly. It is the job of the preacher to remind people to flee the wrath of God.

The unsaved man desperately needs a preacher to cry out: "In flaming fire taking vengeance on them that know not God, and that obey not the gospel of our Lord Jesus Christ: Who shall be punished with everlasting destruction from the presence of the Lord, and from the glory of his power" (2 Thessalonians 1:8-9). The worldly church member lives as he does because few preachers have the courage to say: "The time *is come* that judgment must begin at the house of God: and if *it* first *begin* at us, what shall the end *be* of them that obey not the gospel of God?" (1 Peter 4:17) A profane nation must be told "the wrath of God is revealed from heaven against all ungodliness and unrighteousness of men, who hold the truth in unrighteousness" (Romans 1:18).

It is no accident when the judgment of God falls upon the land. It is the deliberate act of a holy God.

God's judgment is frightening. "I will utterly consume all *things* from off the land, saith the LORD" (Zephaniah 1:2). These words are too powerful, too convicting, and too terrifying for the modern seminary scholars. As they have written their personal Bibles and versions, so they have removed the phrase "utterly consume" and replaced it with a more congenial phrase. Modern ears cannot tolerate such harsh words, so the 'new and improved' Bibles tell the sinner that God will simply "sweep away"[9] the negative.

The Hebrew Bible repeats the verb to demonstrate the totality of the action. It is the reason the word "utterly" is used. The consumption is not partial, it is an annihilation. Such wording ought to drive dread into our hearts for the wrath of God.

The chapter demonstrates the folly of the modern translations. In verse 18, God stated, "the whole land shall be devoured by the fire of his jealousy." Brooms sweep away. Fire consumes. When God was ready to judge the land, He promised to do so with an utterly consuming fire, not a whisk broom.

The various translations of this single verse illustrate the reason modern Bibles have never produced revival. Like the ministers who endorse them, today's translators are on a mission to be certain they never offend. They are not concerned about the purity of God's chosen words but are readily willing to substitute phrases and words carefully chosen to mitigate the wrath of God. They mock and taunt God with their gender-neutral bibles. So careful are they not to offend a lost society, they commit the heinous sin of offending the Holiness of God.

The purpose of Zephaniah's preaching was to alarm and terrorize a people standing on the precipice of the judgment of God. Time was running out, and human sensitivities were not the paramount concern. Revival was the need of the hour, so the man of God does not flinch. "I will consume." "I will cut off." "I will stretch out my hand" (a phrase meaning that God was going to act in a hostile manner against them). When the building is burning down, there is no need for a discussion, nor time to worry about whose feelings are hurt. With the clock striking midnight, the people are in desperate need for the truth.

I recently asked a friend who was attending a soft church if he could remember the last time they had a revival meeting. He said it had been at least ten years. The pastor, who inherited the church from his father, preferred a less confrontational approach. If he cared enough to ask the church members where and when they had been saved, he might have been surprised to find out how many had trusted Christ in a preaching service. If he asked them what kind of preaching convicted them of their sin, he would find out it was hard, powerful preaching. If he asked them what subject convinced them to be saved, he would find out it most likely was a message on Hell or the Judgment of God. Zephaniah would not be welcome in that church, nor would he be tolerated in most churches across the land.

God's judgment is complete. In verse three, the order of creation is reversed. God will destroy "man and beast...the fowls of the heaven...the fishes of the sea". Nothing will be spared. The human creations and inventions that are so impressive in our eyes will be turned into "stumblingblocks" - piles of garbage and rubbish. God would not be impressed that someone lived in the beautiful city of Jerusalem, nor would the fact they were the chosen people of God living in Judah be enough to spare them.

The Day of the Lord's wrath was coming. Listen as He "bid(s) his guests" (Zephaniah 1:7) to come to the dinner of His wrath:

"And it shall come to pass in the day of the LORD'S sacrifice, that I will punish the princes, and the king's children, and all such as are clothed with strange apparel...all those that leap on the threshold, which fill their masters' houses with violence and deceit...all the merchant people...the men that are settled on their lees..." (Zephaniah 1:8-12).

Certainly, God judges "without respect of persons" (1 Peter 1:17). He will call out the princes who lead the government. The children of the king would face the anger of God. It is noted that Zephaniah carefully removed King Josiah from the list of the doomed, but his children would be a different story. Their grandfather and great grandfather lived wretched lives of sin and debauchery, but their own father stood courageously for right. They lived with one of the finest examples of holy living any child has ever been privileged to enjoy, yet Jehoahaz, Jehoiakim, and Zedekiah chose to follow an evil path. They were without excuse when God dealt with them.

God promised to punish worldly Israelites who were clothed in "strange apparel." Wearing the dress of foreigners signified the desire to be like the Assyrians in every way. "The princely households [were] frivolously dazzled by supposed foreign sophistication...the issue at stake was the distinctiveness of the people of God."[10] It was not a very great leap for Judah to go from wanting to dress like the Assyrians to desiring to worship like the Assyrians. "As the people of Judah had adopted the idols of the surrounding nations largely in the hope of gaining political or business advantages, so they adopted also their dress, and were eager to parade the latest fashions from the millinery and tailor shops of Babylon, Nineveh, (and) Memphis."[11]

The wrath of God would descend upon the superstitious who leapt "on the threshold." Pagans believed in the silly notion that evil spirits resided in the thresholds of their doors, waiting for someone to step on it and set them free. They would jump over the threshold so the evil spirits would not get them. Little did they know that the evil spirits were not under their thresholds; they were in their hearts.

In the crosshairs were the workers who were procuring goods by threats, cheating, and fraud. Those merchant men would go to work every morning in the Maktesh district of Jerusalem (the mortar district set aside for business) convinced their riches would solve any problem. They never imagined that the day was coming when the judgment of God would produce crying, howling, and crashing. Their beloved empire would be broken before their eyes and their mighty kingdom would no longer stand.

The complacent, indifferent man would not be spared. He is described in the Bible as a man "settled on (his) lees". In the wine-making process, fermented wine must be poured from one vessel to another to separate the wine from the sediment (lees or 'dregs'). If the wine is allowed to settle too long, it thickens and ruins.[12] So many were oblivious and unconcerned about the abundant idols in the land and a covenant with God that had been shredded. They convinced themselves the "LORD will not do good, neither will he do evil" (Zephaniah 1:12), but they were sadly mistaken.

Some were active in their wickedness, others turned a blind eye to it all, but they would equally face the destruction of God. He promised, "I will search Jerusalem with candles" (Zephaniah 1:12). Invaders would search captured cities with small, clay lamps, looking for any item of value. It would be like taking a flashlight and searching the smallest crevice. When God judged the land, no detail would be too small (Zephaniah 1:13).

He would turn their goods into a booty. The 'stuff' they lived to accumulate would find their way into the pockets of the enemy. They spent their lives building their dream houses but they would never get to inhabit them. That privilege would go to the enemy. Their precious little vineyards that had been carefully cultivated would provide fruit for someone else to eat.

God's judgment would affect every corner of their lives. The man of God had the responsibility of preaching and warning his people of that message. The building was on fire and Zephaniah was shouting.

In April of 1912, Pastor John Harper of the Walworth Road Baptist Church of London, boarded a ship with his six year old daughter headed for the United States. He was planning to go to Chicago for a return preaching engagement at the Moody Memorial Church. His original travel plans placed him on the ocean liner RMS *Lusitania*, a ship which would be torpedoed and sunk by the Germans in 1915, but a last minute schedule change placed him on another boat, the RMS *Titanic*. As the journey began,

Harper was seen on the deck attempting to lead a young man to Christ.

Late in the evening of April 14th, an iceberg scraped the starboard side, showering the decks with ice and ripping a hole in the boat. At first, the passengers were convinced the ship would never sink, but when the alarms began to sound, they scurried to the lifeboats. Harper handed his daughter to an upper deck captain with instructions to get her to safety. His daughter would be among those rescued, while he would be lost attempting to rescue the perishing.

As the freezing waters of the Atlantic engulfed the *Titanic*, Harper could be heard shouting above the screams, "Let the women, children, and the unsaved into the lifeboats!" He gave his life jacket to another assuring his own death.

When Harper was struggling in the icy waters, a wave carried him near a Canadian man clinging to a wooden mast of the ship. He cried out, "Are you saved?" When the man responded he was not, the preacher told him, "Believe on the Lord Jesus Christ and thou shalt be saved!" Before responding, the man drifted into the darkness. When the current brought the man into view, Harper shouted the question again, and begged the man to believe in Christ. As the man was trusting Christ, Harper slipped below the waves and was never seen again. His last act was to lead the man to Christ.[13]

"Let the unsaved into the lifeboats! Believe on the Lord Jesus Christ!" Such are the cries of the man of God when there would be no tomorrow. Such are the cries of a prophet of the Lord like Zephaniah when the hour of

God's judgment is reaching midnight. Such must be the cries of a Bible preacher if we shall ever know revival.

And a young king was listening.

Chapter Five

Revival Preaching and False Religion

AS THE CASE WAS BEING BUILT against the people of Jerusalem, the indictment included a boatload of sins. Isaiah, Jeremiah, Ezekiel, and Micah were but a few of the men of God that listed in detail the specific reasons for the day of reckoning. But whenever the sins are enumerated, there is always one that rises to the top. When the land was finally conquered and despoiled by Nebuchadnezzar, there remained a reason above all reasons God dealt with them.

Israel's great sin was the sin of false religion.

Some eight centuries before Zephaniah prophesied of the indignation of God upon the land, their father Moses stood before God. Handed to Israel on a silver platter was not simply the offer of a lifetime, it was the offer of the ages. The mighty God of eternity was ready to enter into a covenant with them:

"Ye have seen what I did unto the Egyptians, and *how* I bare you on eagles' wings, and brought you unto myself. Now therefore, if ye will obey my voice indeed, and keep my covenant, then ye shall be a peculiar treasure unto me above all people: for all the earth *is* mine: And ye shall be unto me a kingdom of priests, and an holy nation" (Exodus 19:4-6).

How could they say no? It did not take very long before "all the people answered together, and said, All that the LORD hath spoken we will do" (Exodus 19:8). So God responded with Ten Words that He demanded they obey, promising in turn to be their God. In listing those commandments, attention is immediately drawn to the prominent one at the top:

"Thou shalt have no other gods before me" (Exodus 20:3).

In case there was a problem understanding what He meant, He expounded with the second command:

"Thou shalt not make unto thee any graven image, or any likeness *of any thing* that *is* in heaven above, or that *is* in the earth beneath, or that *is* in the water under the earth: Thou shalt not bow down thyself to them, nor serve them: for I the LORD thy God *am* a jealous God, visiting the iniquity of the fathers upon the children unto the third and fourth *generation* of them that hate me; And shewing mercy unto thousands of them that love me, and keep my commandments" (Exodus 20:4-6).

Exodus 21-31 told the children of Israel exactly how they were to worship and honor Him. In total, there are 342 verses in those chapters elucidating to the nation how they were to approach the Holy God of the Bible. When He was done, He gave Moses "two tables of testimony, tables of stone, written with the finger of God" (Exodus 31:18).

The people could not last 40 days. When they saw that God's timeframe differed from theirs, they mocked the mighty God of the Bible by fashioning a molten calf and saying, "These *be* thy gods, O Israel, which brought thee up out of the land of Egypt" (Exodus 32:4). Centuries later, Ezekiel would explain they had learned their false religion from the idolatry of Egypt (Ezekiel 20:8).

Moses descended from Mt. Sinai to judge the people for their great sin. He smashed the idol, demanded they choose sides, and executed the death penalty for those who were intimately responsible for the false god. When he returned to the mountain to meet God, he quickly learned the penalty of bowing down to a false god and worshipping in a false religion. Those who had sinned against God would have their names blotted out of His book (Exodus 32:33). The entire land (most had sinned by ignoring the idol) would be plagued. Then the Lord added words which may have seemed somewhat innocuous to Moses: "nevertheless in the day when I visit I will visit their sin upon them" (Exodus 32:34).

In the chaotic, swirling disasters of that particular day, those words may have quickly made their way to the back burner. There was enough to handle right now without worrying about a future day when God promised to visit their idolatry and false religion upon them. But with the golden calf, the people of Israel had flipped over the hourglass of the wrath of God, and though it would take some 800 years, one day false religion would be paid for.

The sands slipped through the hourglass for centuries. There were a few good kings, but more evil kings. Though the brothers to the north would be conquered and decimated, Jerusalem seemed to stand the test of time. But as an old preacher put it, "God's millstone may turn slowly, but it also turns surely." Payday was coming.

There were but a few grains of sand left in the hourglass when Zephaniah stepped up. He joined the chorus of the prophets of Jehovah in condemning evil religion with these words:

"I will also stretch out mine hand upon Judah, and upon all the inhabitants of Jerusalem; and I will cut off the remnant of Baal from this place, *and* the name of the Chemarims with the priests; And them that worship the host of heaven upon the housetops; and them that worship *and* that swear by the LORD, and that swear by Malcham; And them that are turned back from the LORD; and *those* that have not sought the LORD, nor enquired for him" (Zephaniah 1:4-6).

Despite a history of men like David, Isaiah, Micah, and Hezekiah, there was still a "remnant" that served Baal. Baal was the god of Canaan who allegedly blessed their crops and made the land fertile. When Israel entered into the land of promise, the Canaanites taught them how to farm and live in the land. They also taught them how to worship their pagan god.

Through the centuries, they were often free to be bold in their Baalism. On other occasions, when a good man sat on the throne, they were forced to worship their idols secretly. Even in the days of Zephaniah's preaching, there were those who preferred the Chemarim, the pagan priests that served Baal. Others would make their ways to their flat rooftops and worship the sun and the moon and the stars. Despite a righteous Josiah sitting on the throne, some preferred to worship and serve "the creature more than the Creator" (Romans 1:25).

Worse were the ecumenical compromisers. These spineless scholars would swear by the Lord and swear by Malcham, depending on whom they needed to please, and who, no doubt, paid the most. They followed the path of Aaron, who stood before the golden calf, built an altar, and said, "Tomorrow *is* a feast to the LORD" (Exodus 32:5).

They were like the man living in the days of the Civil War. He had friends and family living in the north, and friends and family living in the south. He really didn't care who won the war, but he did care that everybody liked him. He decided to get himself a gray jacket to please the southerners, and a blue pair of pants to pacify his northern friends. Pleased with himself, he set out from his house.

The north shot him in the heart. The south shot him in the bottom.

Zephaniah opened fire with a trenchant rebuke. These gutless phonies would not have it both ways with the man of God. He exposed their disloyalty to God, proven when they "turned back" and refused to seek Him.

What preaching! When Zephaniah was finished no one wondered what he meant. The sin was exposed, the guilty were unmasked, and the wrath of God was brandished. The people may not have liked what they heard but they had no misconceptions. There was no duplicity in this prophet of the Lord!

America is full of ministers straddling the fence. One message is preached before the Sunday morning parishioners, but a very different lecture is delivered in the seminary classroom. One sermon is tailored for the 'contemporary' service at 10 am, another for the 'traditional' service at 11.

No wonder there is no respect! No wonder there is no repentance! No wonder there is no revival!

A man of God like Zephaniah puts the blinders on. He is not seeking the popularity of the crowd, the ministerial fellowship, or his favorite professor. He is crying out with the Apostle Paul, "For do I now persuade men, or God? or do I seek to please men? for if I yet pleased men, I should not be the servant of Christ" (Galatians 1:10). The preaching is plain and pointed, so no one leaves the building wondering what he meant.

The comedian Bill Cosby was once asked the secret of success. He responded, "I am afraid I do not know the key to success. I do, however, know the key to failure. It is trying to please everyone."[14]

America's preachers have followed the political correctness of our era, fearing to preach plainly lest their words offend. But there is a very old book telling of a mighty prophet that preached revival down. He did not leave the people guessing. He spelled it out for them.

And a young king was listening.

Chapter Six

The Urgency of Revival Preaching

ON JUNE 17, 1963, the United States Supreme Court, by an 8-1 verdict, tossed the Bible out of the public schools of America. Ground zero was Abington Township, Pennsylvania, a stately suburb of Philadelphia. Edward Schempp, a Universalist Unitarian, along with the able assistance of the ACLU, brought the case on behalf of his son Ellery. Though Schempp was offended that the state of Pennsylvania had mandatory Bible readings in the classroom, he was not offended that his son read the Koran in the same class.

He certainly was ahead of the times.

In reporting the story for the evening news, a major network sent a crew to a public elementary school in Abington Township. The story they narrated that day has certainly had its consequences. In a recent year, the Department of Education reported that 1,183,700 violent crimes were committed at America's public schools. Violent crimes include "rape, sexual battery other than rape, physical attack or fight with or without a weapon, threat of physical attack with or without a weapon, and robbery with or without a weapon".[15]

At least no one is being offended by the Ten Commandments.

Over time, the township closed the very school that hosted the news crew, and the once proud, stone building was sold and left to decay.

The Bible says, "God is not mocked" (Galatians 6:7). One day, a pastor named Mel Hall approached the owner of that very building with an offer from his young congregation to purchase it. Today the very place where America heard that its schools could no longer teach the Bible is the home of Calvary Baptist Church. God reminds us yet again, "Heaven and earth shall pass away, but my words shall not pass away" (Matthew 24:35).

There are mountains of evidence proving the authority of the Bible as the very written Words of God. One of its great demonstrations is on display in Zephaniah 1:14-17, a passage describing the 'Day of the Lord'. An in depth study of the Day of the Lord is intriguing to be sure, and such an examination would send a student on a journey covering every corner of the Bible. 27 of the 66 books in the Bible deal with the subject. It is a broad topic covering a great timeframe which will effect every individual who has ever lived on the earth.

In many of the passages, such as the text in Zephaniah 1, the Day of the Lord has a two-fold meaning. There was an immediate interpretation for the prophet Zephaniah, King Josiah, and the citizens of Judah. There is also a long term purpose applying to people who would be born 25 centuries after the prophet had died.

Pastor David Sorenson put it like this:

It is clear that the immediate context of Zephaniah 1 is of the impending invasion and destruction of Jerusalem at the hand of Babylon. However, there seems to be a shift in the focus here. The term the day of the Lord is otherwise used in the Bible to refer to events at the end of the church age and the time of Christ's return. In short, it usually refers to the Tribulation and the Millennium (and the eternal kingdom as well). It is a time when God will seize the reins of human history and in effect says, 'I am taking over now!'[16]

Only the living God of the Bible could produce such a book! When one stops to think that the Bible has not only stood the test of time (more than 3 millennia), but that it remains a part of everyday life for millions of people, it truly is remarkable. It is not a relic. It is a miracle book produced by a mighty God. It was 100% relevant in the day of Zephaniah. It is 100% relevant today.

The prophet Zephaniah was convinced that judgment was imminent. There was no time to run and hide. It was time to "Hold thy peace at the presence of the Lord GOD" (Zephaniah 1:7). There was no place for human reason or opinion. In the presence of the Lord GOD (the divine personal name and the powerful mighty name of God) every human will be silenced. That terror motivated him to toss aside the normal ministerial style and replace it with a desperate cry:

"The great day of the LORD is near, it is near, and hasteth greatly, even the voice of the day of the LORD: the mighty man shall cry there bitterly. That day is a day of wrath, a day of trouble and distress, a day of wasteness and desolation, a day of darkness and gloominess, a day of clouds and thick darkness, A day of the trumpet and alarm against the fenced cities, and against the high towers. And I will bring distress upon men, that they shall walk like blind men, because they have sinned against the LORD: and their blood shall be poured out as dust, and their flesh as the dung. Neither their silver nor their gold shall be able to deliver them in the day of the LORD'S wrath; but the whole land shall be devoured by the fire of his jealousy: for he shall make even a speedy riddance of all them that dwell in the land" (Zephaniah 1:14-17).

Revival preaching recognizes the imminency of the Day of God's judgment and responds accordingly. The preacher is so overwhelmed with the Holiness of God and the wickedness of humanity he cannot help but cry out passionately. There is no place for a dull monotone when one preaches like Zephaniah. The verses cannot be read dispassionately, for each word is loaded with power and dread driving the listener to the brink of decision.

The fear in Zephaniah's voice is palpable. "The day of the LORD *is* at hand...(it) *is* near, *it is* near, and hasteth greatly". As we do not know the day nor the hour, neither did Zephaniah. The end was closing in on Jerusalem and within fifty years Nebuchadnezzar and his forces would demolish the city. He didn't know the exact time on the clock of judgment, but when listening to him preach, one is left with the impression there were but fifty seconds left.

Zephaniah tells them what to listen for. In the day of God's wrath the mightiest soldiers will "cry bitterly". That 'cry' is a war-cry, a loud shrill. The Day will be so horrible that the warrior of many battles, accustomed to blood-curdling scenes and horrifying destruction, will shriek in abject terror at this unprecedented devastation.[17]

Zephaniah tells them what to look for. The word 'day' is used six times. In six days, God created the heaven and the earth. What God builds He is able to destroy. The ultimate end of the Day of the Lord will be a new heaven and a new earth.

1. *It is a "day of wrath."* It expresses an overwhelming and complete demonstration of God's anger upon a deserving earth. His wrath "burns, overflows, sweeps away everything before it... nothing stands."[18] Everyone and everything that has opposed him will melt like silver in a fiery furnace (Ezekiel 22:22).

2. *It is a "day of trouble and distress."* These words in the Hebrew language are powerful and poetic, painting a picture of anguish and fear.

3. *It is a "day of wasteness and desolation."* When God is finished the land will look like a barren badlands barely able to tell the story of its past.

4. *It is a "darkness and gloominess."* The preacher goes from telling what will happen to them to what is happening around them. As Isaiah and Amos and Joel prophesied, a fearful blackness will envelop the earth.

5. ***It is a "day of clouds and thick darkness."*** The God who created the earth in six days is bringing it back to its original state. One can picture the "black thunderclouds, from which flash forth the lightning bolts of the Lord's fierce wrath." [19]

6. ***It is a "day of the trumpet and alarm."*** Like the sirens in a midwestern city screaming of an approaching killer tornado, the alarms sound the coming attack of the enemies. The God who once fought for them (Numbers 10:9) was now fighting against them.

Zephaniah tells them why. They "have sinned against the LORD". Their sin was not against each other but rather a rebellion against their Creator, and He was paying them back. They shut their eyes to the Word of God so He made them permanently blind. Because they cheapened life, their blood would be no better than the dust of the field and their flesh they so honored would rot like dung.

Zephaniah tells them what won't work. God will not be impressed with "their silver nor their gold". There is a double meaning here. Their dead idols of silver and gold would not be able to save them from the living God. For those who made money their idol, they would discover that God is not for sale. Their money may have bought men and possessions, but it will never purchase deliverance.

They had mocked God for the final time, and now the "fire of his jealousy" would speak for Him. The jealousy of God was an intense desire to honor His name and reputation. He simply would not allow His glory to be despised and dragged through the world's mud, so now, with great speed, He would deal with the land. Time was running out and Zephaniah knew it.

When will America's preachers sound like Zephaniah? As God described the imminent wrath to fall upon an unrepentant Jerusalem in his day, we have a multitude of verses describing the Great Tribulation ready to fall on our world. The 'twinkling of an eye' is the only thing separating this world from the Day of God's wrath cascading upon a helpless world. It will look like this:

"And the kings of the earth, and the great men, and the rich men, and the chief captains, and the mighty men, and every bondman, and every free man, hid themselves in the dens and in the rocks of the mountains; And said to the mountains and rocks, Fall on us, and hide us from the face of him that sitteth on the throne, and from the wrath of the Lamb: For the great day of his wrath is come; and who shall be able to stand?" (Revelation 6:15-17)

If that weren't enough, the sinner without Christ is one heartbeat away from the fires of Hell. Every breath, every moment of his life is encompassed by the dire words of John 3:36: "and he that believeth not the Son shall not see life; but the wrath of God abideth on him." It is not that the lost sinner will in the future face the wrath of God, but rather, God's anger is hanging over his immortal soul right now. How is it possible that a man who claims to believe the Bible can not lift up his voice and warn the sinner to flee the wrath to come?

Arguably the most famous sermon ever preached in America was *"Sinners in the Hands of an Angry God,"* a message delivered in Enfield, Connecticut, by Jonathan Edwards. The city was previously unaffected by the Great Awakening, and the crowd that gathered on that Saturday in 1741 was rather nonchalant. The preacher opened his Bible to Deuteronomy 32:35 and read, "To me *belongeth* vengeance, and recompence; their foot shall slide in *due* time: for the day of their calamity *is* at hand, and the things that shall come upon them make haste."

He continued:

"As he that walks in slippery places is every moment liable to fall, he cannot foresee one moment whether he shall stand or fall the next; and when he does fall, he falls at once without warning…the bow of God's wrath is bent, and the arrow made ready on the string, and justice bends the arrow at your heart, and strains the bow, and it is nothing but the mere pleasure of God, and that of an angry God, without any promise or obligation at all, that keeps the arrow one moment from being made drunk with your blood. Thus all you that have never passed under a great change of heart, by the mighty power of the Spirit of God upon your souls; all you that were never born again, and made new creatures, and raised from being dead in sin, to a state of new, and before altogether unexperienced light and life, are in the hands of an angry God.

"Let everyone that is out of Christ now awake and fly from the wrath to come. The wrath of Almighty God is now undoubtedly hanging over a great part of this congregation. Let everyone fly

out of Sodom: 'Haste and escape for your lives, look not behind you, escape to the mountain, lest you be consumed.'"

His message was interrupted by screaming people begging him to stop. Others were crying out, "What must I do to be saved?" It was so overwhelming, Edwards had to stop speaking until the crowd quieted. When he was done Enfield would not be the same.[20]

Revival preaching impresses the listener with the impending wrath of God and the pressing need to be right with God right now. Have we become so hardened and calloused that we no longer care? Are we so entrenched in our methods and programs that we are incapable of seeing where this road is going? Do we lack the courage to preach the truth and fear the consequences of human rejection?

And a young king was listening.

Chapter Seven

Revival Preaching Pleads

IN THE DAYS of the Revolutionary War, a Baptist preacher named Peter Miller served in Ephrata, Pennsylvania. Near his church lived a man who incessantly maligned the pastor. The same man committed an act of treason, was arrested, and sentenced to be hanged. The preacher started out on foot, walking 70 miles to Philadelphia to beg for the man's life. George Washington heard him, and said, "No, your plea for your friend cannot be granted." "My friend!" said the preacher. "He is the worst enemy I have." "What!" said Washington. "You have walked nearly seventy miles to save the life of an enemy? That puts the matter in a different light. I will grant the pardon."[21]

In Zephaniah 2, the man of God moved from preaching to pleading. The overwhelming urgency of the Day of the Lord, and the impending doom of God's judgment dominated his message, yet it is in vain without a message informing people of God's expectations. There is an answer. It is late, but it is not yet too late:

"Gather yourselves together, yea, gather together, O nation not desired; Before the decree bring forth, before the day pass as the chaff, before the fierce anger of the LORD come upon you, before the day of the LORD'S anger come upon you. Seek ye the LORD, all ye meek of the earth, which have wrought his judgment; seek righteousness, seek meekness: it may be ye shall be hid in the day of the LORD'S anger" (Zephaniah 2:1-3)

God wanted them to "gather together, yea, gather together." The command is so critical it is repeated. One can hear the trepidation in Zephaniah's voice, for he realized that the number of invitations was limited.

The word was commonly used to describe the gathering of wheat at the time of harvest. Indeed, the harvest of God's judgment was ready to fall upon Judah, so He called them to an assembly. Zephaniah acted as a spokesman for God informing them their wickedness had made them a nation "not desired." It was unusual for God to call His people a "nation," but He is now equating them with the pagan people surrounding them.

They were running out of time, so Zephaniah told them to repent and do it in a hurry. Usually, we are ready to get right with God *after* the judgment. *After* the enemy strikes, *after* the tornado destroys, *after* the earth quakes, we as humans are finally ready to listen to the Word of God. We find time for God *after* our world unravels.

But the preacher is telling them there won't be time *after*. He said to gather and make time for God *"before* the decree bring forth," *"before* the day pass as the chaff," *"before* the fierce anger of the Lord come upon you." The last phrase is repeated, a method of describing God's wrath as coming again and again, relentlessly hitting them from all sides. The moment God would issue the decree of judgment He would separate the wheat from the chaff, and the hour for gathering, preaching, and repenting would be gone.

It is astounding to witness the attitude of churches in our day. As we march ever closer to the Day of the Lord, billowing clouds of judgment rise on the horizon. Our nation is mocking God and His word. In our lifestyles, our entertainment, our politics, our priorities, we are removing God and placing ourselves on the throne. We stand on the precipice of the righteous judgment of God cascading upon our land, and how do churches respond?

They are canceling services.

Prayer meeting is replaced by aerobics classes. Youth Bible studies are replaced by rock concerts. Sunday night services are replaced by football parties. Revival meetings are replaced by self-help classes.

How unwelcome Zephaniah would be in the modern church! To insist that people "gather together" for preaching is so 'Old Testament'! It is so 'legalistic'!

But there is this little verse in the 'New Testament:' "Not forsaking the assembling of ourselves together, as the manner of some *is*; but exhorting *one another*: and so much the more, as ye see the day approaching" (Hebrews 10:25). Not less preaching, "so much the more" preaching. Not less Bible, "so much the more" Bible. Not less conviction, "so much the more" conviction.

This is not the day to stay home and watch TV. This is the day to "gather yourselves together" in the New Testament local church, to tremble before the Holy God of the Bible, and to repent of our wickedness, for the day is fast approaching when it will be too late.

God wanted them to "seek...seek...seek". Zephaniah told the people to invest their time learning what God desires and then living to please Him. The repetition of the word implies that seeking and pleasing Him is not a one time event. One cannot seek the Lord for an hour on Sunday morning and then forget about Him the remainder of the week.

If we are truly seeking Him, we are doing so on His terms. A seeker is not telling God how He is to be honored and worshipped. A seeker is not so audacious to think that he gets to set the rules. A seeker humbly invests his life in finding out how to please God, and then obeying.

God wanted them to be meek people. At this critical juncture in Jerusalem's history, it was the humble people of the city that had set the stage for revival. Tired of the evil reigns of amoral kings, they coronated an 8 year old boy. Imagine the response of the neighboring nations to such a move. But the man of God encouraged them with the reminder that they didn't need an impressive king, a powerful king, or a worldly king, as much as they needed a godly king.

Meek people are concerned about obeying God's judgment and righteousness. Their only hope was a leader that would be just and equal in his dealings, obedient to the God of Israel. More than a century earlier, the prophet

Hosea leveled this warning: "And the pride of Israel testifieth to his face: And they do not return to the Lord their God, nor seek him for all this" (Hosea 7:10). They finally understood that the obstinate arrogance of a narcissistic leader absorbed with human hubris would only destroy the land.

We have come a long way from the days of George Washington bowing his knees and his heart on the snowy ground of Valley Forge, Pennsylvania. When Abraham Lincoln walked the streets of Richmond, Virginia, a newly freed group of slaves cried out, "Glory Hallelujah" and bowed their knees to the president. He quickly responded, "Don't kneel to me…kneel only to God!"[22] When someone asked Ronald Reagan if he was aware of all the people who were praying for him, he responded,"Yes I am. I believe in intercessory prayer." Then he added these words: "Sometimes when you were praying you may have gotten a busy signal. It was just me in there ahead of you."[23]

It is mighty hard to find politicians in Washington seeking righteousness and meekness. Then again, it is mighty hard to find people in the land seeking righteousness and meekness. Perhaps the two are more related than we think.

God wanted them to understand the essence of time. A century earlier, when Amos was crying out to the people of Israel to turn from their wicked ways, the prophet said, "Seek the Lord and live, or he will sweep through the house of Joseph like a fire" (Amos 5:6). That was a direct and unqualified promise. If the people would seek God, then the fire of judgment would not come and they would live.[24]

The promise of Amos becomes the possibility of Zephaniah. 100 years down the highway of idolatry and immorality meant the fraying thread was nearing its last strand. Now, God would only say "it may be ye shall be hid in the day of the LORD's anger." Even the humble, righteous citizens were in danger of being swallowed up by the wrath of God. The certainty had turned into a "it may be." The clock was striking midnight, and even those who feared God would not escape the calamity. God's invitation was not interminable.

And a young king was listening.

Chapter Eight
Revival Preaching and the Choir

I HAVE DISCOVERED there are certain sins that are popular to preach against in local churches. We can preach against the sins of Washington, the sins of the abortionists, the sins of corrupt judges, the sins of Hollywood, the sins of the sodomites, and pretty much any sin 'out there' as long as it is not 'in here.'

And people love it.

The weakest of ministers have somebody in their crosshairs they can preach against, and that is normally enough to convince the parishioners that they are taking a strong stand against sin. The little secret is that a lot of money can be raised if you are against the right things. People like a minister that agrees with them on the social issue of the day, and there is a lot of support for someone that stands against 'those' sins. It is easy to preach to the choir.

Not many preach against the choir.

The preaching of Zephaniah is masterful. With the exception of Hosea, every one of the prophets in the back of the Old Testament preached messages of judgment against foreign nations. With flourish and colorful word pictures, men like Obadiah, Amos, and Jonah preached the wrath of God that would fall on pagan lands. Zephaniah joined the club covering every point on the compass.

He starts out west, exposing the sins of the Philistines. Though there had been many a skirmish between Israel and Philistia through the corridor of time, they still found a way to coexist for more than 500 years. The Philistines had their fishing businesses and the Jews their crops. But there was a history of conflict, and a preacher condemning them would certainly be a popular man. Zephaniah did not let them down.

In 711 BC, the city of Gath had been conquered by the Assyrians, leaving four major cities in the territory. Each one had a special promise from the man of God. Lying some fifty miles to the southwest of Jerusalem was the city of Gaza. Zephaniah promised they would be "forsaken" (Zephaniah 2:4). Ashkelon was to become a "desolation," a ghost town. Both of these cities had a coming appointment with mighty King Nebuchadnezzar and would not last twenty years.

There may have been some chuckles when Zephaniah prophesied that Ashdod would be driven out "at the noon day." When the Egyptians tried to conquer the city they had to lay siege against it for twenty-nine long years, but God promised to destroy the city and be home in time for lunch. Like a woman in the garden rooting out a weed,

God would deal with the city of Ekron. Their houses and villages would become "cottages for shepherds and folds for flocks," (Zephaniah 2:6) a great disgrace for a nation that despised sheep.

Zephaniah looked to the east and preached judgment against Moab and Ammon. These descendants of Lot were constantly fighting Israel, with Kings and Chronicles recording seven different texts describing the battles. Isaiah, Amos, Jeremiah, and Ezekiel denounced them in nine distinct messages.

Zephaniah called them out: "I have heard the reproach of Moab, and the revilings of the children of Ammon, whereby they have reproached my people, and magnified *themselves* against their border" (Zephaniah 2:8). They had scorned, disgraced, and insulted their half brothers one time too many and their words of slander reached the ears of Almighty God. Little did they know they were actually taunting the people who belonged to "the LORD of hosts" (Zephaniah 2:10).

So God raises His Hand and makes an oath: "Therefore *as* I live, saith the LORD of hosts, the God of Israel" (Zephaniah 2:9). Dead idols cannot swear upon their own lives for they have no life. But the living God of the Bible is ready to go to war. When God makes such an oath, humans are in serious trouble.

God promised: "Surely Moab shall be as Sodom, and the children of Ammon as Gomorrah." Those words should have stunned them, for they were actually born out of the destruction of Sodom and Gomorrah. 1200 years earlier, their father Lot fled for his life from the smoking cities, ultimately landing in a desolate cave degrading his daughters. From that incestuous relationship the Ammonites and Moabites were born.

Their own eyes could tell them what became of Sodom: "the breeding of nettles, and saltpits, and a perpetual desolation." 2600 years later, our eyes can see the same thing. The man of God promised they would wind up at the place they started. This would be the payment for their "pride, because they have reproached and magnified *themselves* against the people of the LORD." They picked a fight with God, and now He would be "terrible unto them" (Zephaniah 2:11).

Zephaniah looks to the south with a brief message: "Ye Ethiopians also, ye *shall be* slain by my sword" (Zephaniah 2:12). To the people of Zephaniah's day, Ethiopia, the territory south of Egypt, was the end of the world. Such a pronouncement told the people that God's wrath knew no bounds.

There was a message to the Assyrian power to the north and its main city of Nineveh. They ruled that part of the world for more than a century causing more than one sleepless night for Israel and its kings. They were famous for their brutality in conquering their foes. Though their power was waning as Josiah took the throne, they were still a formidable foe.

They surely terrorized their enemies, but they did not frighten God. He promised to "stretch out his hand against the north, and destroy Assyria; and...make Nineveh a desolation, *and* dry like a wilderness" (Zephaniah 2:13). Zephaniah joins the prophet Nahum in prophesying the demise of their great enemy, a message that must have seemed too good to be true.

Zephaniah preached that God would dry them up, a significant prediction for a city on the Tigris River that was full of canals. They had what they believed was an endless water supply but God promised to make them dry "like a wilderness." For generations the armies of Assyria had returned from battles with marvelous spoils of conquered people creating a people who lived "carelessly," but now their riches would become a "desolation." Most importantly, their arrogance was about to meet the anger of God head on. They would boast, "I am" (Zephaniah 2:14). They were claiming the power, glory, and singular authority that belonged to God alone, and He would not stand for it. His retribution was so complete that people could only pass by, hiss, and wave their hand.

It would not be hard to imagine the building crowd smiling and giving a hearty 'amen' at such a declaration. After all, the Assyrians were despised. Listening to Zephaniah preach must have been an event in itself, for he speaks using verbs in the perfect tense. He must have sounded more like a news reporter describing a breaking disaster, than a prophet of future events. To the man of God, there was no doubt.

Some listeners may have thought the words of Zephaniah were the delusions of a wild-eyed prophet, for no one in the decade of the 620's BC could have seen it coming. The preaching may have been encouraging and entertaining as people imagined the fall of the mighty army to the north, but it must have seemed equally preposterous. Nineveh was too strong:

The city was the world's largest. It had an inner city and an outer city, and these were probably augmented greatly by suburban development. The inner city was surrounded by a wall eight miles in circumference. It was 100 feet high and was so wide that three chariots could have raced around it abreast. It had twelve hundred towers and fourteen gates. Another mighty wall surrounded most of the outer city. At the heart of the city was King Sennacherib's "Palace with No Rival." Lions of bronze and bulls of white marble guarded it. Its great hall measured 150 by 40 feet. Nearby was a 46-acre armory where the king kept his chariots, armor, horses, and other military equipment. Nineveh was an awesome and seemingly impregnable metropolis.[25]

Yet they fell in the lifetime of Zephaniah in the year 612 BC. 211 years later a Greek historian, Xenophon, passed the site of Nineveh and could not find a trace of its existence in the shifting desert sands.[26] How accurate are the promises of God.

Our Bibles put a break between chapters two and three, but there was no break in the preaching of Zephaniah. He deftly moves from the end of Assyria to another topic, and I wonder if the crowd even caught it at first. Hammering the nations that were troubling Israel was a popular message to deliver, but a transition was quick in coming. With the 'amens' resounding off the walls of the city, Zephaniah turns it right back on the people. The target becomes "the oppressing city!" (Zephaniah 3:1).

The article "the" is quite important. "The" city is the city that had a Bible; "the" city that had the sacrifice; "the" city of David. It was "the" city that should have known better.

Zephaniah 1:2 leaves no doubt: "She obeyed not the voice; she received not correction; she trusted not in the LORD; she drew not near to her God." The target of the preacher is no longer living on distant shores. Zephaniah is looking into their eyeballs.

One of the mightiest preachers I have been privileged to know was Richard Anderson. Brother Anderson, who is now in heaven, pastored two churches in northern New Hampshire. He was a fearless man of God who valiantly defended the Word of God and exemplified uncommon courage in preaching.[27]

He often told me this: "I am not as much interested in what a man will preach about, as I am interested in what he *won't* preach about." Well said.

Zephaniah might add: "I am not as much interested in whom a man will preach against, as I am interested in whom he *won't* preach against." Many preachers will condemn the crowd that will never hear them, but Zephaniah turned the pulpit around and preached straight to the choir.

And a young king was listening.

Chapter Nine

Revival Preaching Condemns Sin

FOR MORE THAN 50 years, the angelic voice of Robert Schuller emanated from Garden Grove, California. Not only did he speak to a large congregation, but he also became a television star with more than 1500 episodes broadcast to the world.

Jesus had something to say about ministers like Robert Schuller. "Beware of false prophets, which come to you in sheep's clothing, but inwardly they are ravening wolves" (Matthew 7:15). His success was built on delivering a popular message of "Possibility Thinking." One of his many bestselling books was entitled "Self Esteem - the New Reformation." In the book, he deceives the readers with this definition of sin:

"What do I mean by sin? Answer: Any human condition or act that robs God of glory by stripping one of his children of their right to divine dignity...I can offer still another answer: Sin is any act or thought that robs myself or another human being of his or her self-esteem." He goes on: "Classical theology defines sin as rebellion against God. This answer is not correct as much as it is shallow and insulting to the human being."[28]

How different is the Reverend Robert Schuller from the prophet Zephaniah:

"Woe to her that is filthy and polluted, to the oppressing city! She obeyed not the voice; she received not correction; she trusted not in the LORD; she drew not near to her God. Her princes within her *are* roaring lions; her judges *are* evening wolves; they gnaw not the bones till the morrow. Her prophets *are* light *and* treacherous persons: her priests have polluted the sanctuary, they have done violence to the law" (Zephaniah 3:1-4).

The man of God has a responsibility to name sin - not rename sin. Zephaniah looked at the desperate condition of the people and exposed them, calling them filthy, and polluted oppressors. Doubtlessly, the people convinced themselves they were not warmongers like the Assyrians were, but God saw their violence.

They stubbornly refused to obey the voice of God. Zephaniah said they had heard the voice of God but then rejected it, making them worse than the pagan nations that never heard Him in the first place. They had far more revelations from God than any other nation in world history but they simply dismissed them. When God tried to chasten them they refused to respond.

They lived in unbelief refusing to trust in the Lord. There are multiple verses in the Old Testament where God made wonderful promises to Israel if they would simply heed Him, but they were not interested. "Trust and Obey" was not in their songbook, and their faithlessness was demonstrated by their unwillingness to draw near to God. Everywhere they turned in Jerusalem there were physical reminders of God, multiple feast days and sacrifices that spoke of His mercies and provision, but they did not care.

Zephaniah called out the guilty leadership as well. He named the princes "roaring lions" because they preyed on the people they were supposed to help. The judges were like wolves prowling in the evening. By the time the sun would rise in the morning there was nothing left but bones. The prophets lacked the discipline necessary to represent God to the people, and with their casual attitude to the truth of God, they could not be trusted. Like the sons of Aaron and Eli, the priests in Zephaniah's day were polluters. They tore the Bible to shreds by allowing unholy and pagan elements into the house of God.

It probably would be safe to assume that Zephaniah was not the lead speaker at the National Day of Prayer in Jerusalem.

God placed His woe upon the people and leadership who were hardened. When the ministers refused to condemn sin, and the political leadership became rich off the sin, the common people simply engaged in wicked activity without considering the commands of God.

It is very dangerous when a nation defies the God of the Bible by softening sin and its effects. In our lifetimes, we have witnessed the same compromise:

The word 'values' has replaced 'morals.'
The word 'mistake' has replaced 'sin.'

The word 'affair' has replaced 'adultery.'
The word 'gay' has replaced 'sodomy.'
The phrase 'lose virginity' has replaced 'fornication.'
The phrase 'alternate lifestyle' has replaced 'immorality.'
The word 'alcoholic' has replaced 'drunk.'
The phrase 'substance abuse' has replaced 'drug addict.'
The phrase 'happy hour' has replaced 'drunkenness.'
The word 'choice' has replaced 'murder.'

Foolish humans convince themselves that by changing the name of sin they can change the results of sin, but God told Zephaniah that He will not change with the shifting sands of society:

"The just LORD is in the midst thereof; he will not do iniquity: every morning doth he bring his judgment to light, he faileth not; but the unjust knoweth no shame. I have cut off the nations: their towers are desolate; I made their streets waste, that none passeth by: their cities are destroyed, so that there is no man, that there is none inhabitant. I said, Surely thou wilt fear me, thou wilt receive instruction; so their dwelling should not be cut off, howsoever I punished them: but they rose early, and corrupted all their doings" (Zephaniah 3:5-7).

Humans hide their sin under the cover of darkness but the "just LORD *is* in the midst thereof." We are told that as society changes, right and wrong must adjust. The profane media magnate, Ted Turner, took it upon himself to eliminate the Ten Commandments and replace them with 'ten voluntary initiatives.' Parroting Robert Schuller, he "lambasted fundamentalist Christianity's tenet that man is born into sin, and said Jesus would likely be 'sick at his stomach' over such 'twisted' interpretations of his teachings."[29]

His 'initiatives':

1. I love and respect planet Earth and all living things thereon, especially my fellow species, mankind.

2. I promise to treat all persons everywhere with dignity, respect and friendliness.

3. I promise to have no more than two children, or no more than my nation suggests.

4. I promise to use my best efforts to help save what is left of our natural world in an untouched state and to restore damaged or destroyed areas where practical.

5. I pledge to use as little non-renewable resources as possible.

6. I pledge to use as little toxic chemicals, pesticides and other poisons as possible.

7. I promise to contribute to those less fortunate than myself to help them become self-sufficient and enjoy the benefits of a decent life, including clean air and water, adequate food, health care, housing, education and individual rights.

8. I reject the use of force, in particular military force, and back United Nations arbitration of international disputes.

9. I support the total elimination of all nuclear, chemical and biological weapons, and, in time, the total elimination of all weapons of mass destruction.

10. I support the United Nations in its efforts to collectively improve the conditions of the planet.

God is in the midst of it all. He is not impressed by the degrees of a humanist professor, nor does he tremble before an arrogant politician. Every morning His justice is brought to light as He stands perfect in holiness. To the prophet Zephaniah, He sounded a warning that should cause us to tremble yet today. "I have cut off the nations…I made their streets waste…their cities are destroyed, so that there is no man, that there is none inhabitant…I rise up to the prey: for my determination *is* to gather the nations, that I may assemble the kingdoms, to pour upon them mine indignation, *even* all my fierce anger: for all the earth shall be devoured with the fire of my jealousy" (Zephaniah 3:6, 8).

"I rise up to the prey!" Through the corridor of time the tender patience of God has extended amazing mercies to the wicked, but there always came a time when God rose up and defended His honor. Ask Sodom. Ask Pharaoh. Ask Babylon. The false minister who preaches a trendy gospel and the arrogant humanist who mocks the holy Word of God will witness the day that God rises in indignation (the intense anger of God). They will experience first hand His fierce anger (the word picture describes snorting nostrils) and the fire of His jealousy. There will come a day when those who preyed will be preyed upon and their taunting will haunt them for eternity in the raging lake of fire and brimstone.

They challenged God so He challenged them. "Wait ye upon me" (Zephaniah 3:8). In most of the Biblical occasions where God tells people to wait for Him, He is encouraging the righteous to hold on while reminding them He still cares. But that is not the intent in this verse. God is not telling them to wait until He fixes things. He is saying, "When you think that sinners are getting away with it, just wait for me. You haven't seen anything yet."

Preachers are told to turn down the rhetoric. They step in the pulpit fearful of offending, and should the text they read describe the wrath of God, they apologize to the audience. The weekly message is a blend of positive verses and hopeful psychology, but there will never be revival without repentance. There will never be repentance without preaching that names sin.

The southern preacher R. G. Lee once preached a message in which he was hard and heavy against sin. After the message an irate woman said, "Dr. Lee, I didn't like that sermon!" Dr. Lee replied, "Neither did the devil, sister."[30]

So Zephaniah boldly calls out sin and the sinners, unconcerned about the opinions of the people.

And a young king was listening.

Chapter Ten

The Song of Revival Preaching

ONE OF THE BLESSINGS of evangelism is enjoying wonderful music that honors the Lord. Most churches save their best music for revival meetings, and the singing does a great job of preparing the hearts of people. A good song service can help folks put aside the distractions of the world and focus on the preaching to come. 99.9% of the time, the music is a great blessing.

Years ago, I was preaching in a western state where the 0.1% came into play. It was a Sunday morning service, the first preaching service of the meeting, and a gentleman stood up to sing. The words went like this:

I asked an old time preacher how revival came back there,
He said we always started down on our knees in prayer,
Just open up the two books, the song book and the Bible,
If you sing and preach the word you'll have a revival.[31]

That frivolous song demonstrates the lax thinking that people have about revival. The song book is not a prerequisite for revival, nor is the song book on par with the Bible. When Josiah was used of God to bring revival to the land, he had them stand before the Bible as it was read. It was the reading of the Bible that produced brokenness and repentance. It was the Bible that exposed their sin. It was the Bible that drove them to their knees in seeking God.

The revival of Josiah was a direct result of the recovery of the Bible and the national reading of it. The people repented before God and it set a series of reactions in Jerusalem. The abominations were removed; the passover was kept; the priests were encouraged in the service of the Lord; the offerings were given willingly; the singers were in their place (2 Chronicles 35:1-19).

Music will not produce revival, but music is a great by-product of revival. Zephaniah describes that coming day when the Lord will reign over all the earth, and though it begins as a time of immense judgment, it culminates with 1000 years of glorious hope and blessing to the earth. That day will be a time of singing and shouting:

"Sing, O daughter of Zion; shout, O Israel; be glad and rejoice with all the heart, O daughter of Jerusalem. The LORD hath taken away thy judgments, he hath cast out thine enemy: the king of Israel, *even* the LORD, *is* in the midst of thee: thou shalt not see evil any more. In that day it shall be said to Jerusalem, Fear thou not: *and to* Zion, Let not thine hands be slack" (Zephaniah 3:14-16).

Only the Word of God can take a book full of judgment, wrath, and trouble, and conclude with a magnificent song. It is the song of the Kingdom; the song of the Millennium. The first words from the mouth of the prophet warned people of the consuming wrath of God, but the concluding words left them with the 'song of the soul set free.' When King Jesus sits on His throne there will be a lot of reasons to sing!

We will sing because the "LORD hath taken away thy judgments." The conclusion to a book full of retribution reminds us that God will no longer deal harshly with those He loves. Through the ages of time the Mercy of God and Holiness of God seemed to oppose each other. The battle normally ended with the wrath of God finally erupting on deserving sinners, yet when the final round concludes, Holiness and Mercy will both win out.

When the Millennial song gets to the second verse we will glorify the Savior that has "cast out thine enemy." The words describe a courtroom where God has sentenced Satan and His people are free. The oppression is forever gone, the last battle has been fought, and the great enemy will spend the Millennium in a bottomless pit (Revelation 20:3).

The third verse is even better. "The king of Israel, *even* the LORD, *is* in the midst of thee." One of the king's many responsibilities is to defend the people, and with the King of Kings in the midst of His people it will be impossible for evil to stand. In Israel's past, a pillar represented a manifestation of God. One day He will personally dwell among them. Today the eyes of faith tells us that Jesus dwells in us. One day, the eyes of our head will allow us to look upon Him.

The final verse of the song reminds the people that they "shalt not see evil any more." The fear is forever gone, replaced by the person of Jesus Christ. We do not have the capacity to understand the setting when the saints of the ages gather in Jerusalem to coronate Jesus as the King of the whole world. The glory and majesty of the Creator of the universe will be exalted as the saints who love His name will finally give Him the honor He is due. What a day that will be!

A young boy once complained to his father that most of the church hymns were boring to him. His father put an end to the discussion when he said, "If you think you can write better hymns, then why don't you?" The boy went to his room and wrote his first hymn. This was in 1690; the teenager's name was Isaac Watts.[32]

Three decades later he published a unique hymnal in which the songs were Old Testament Psalms as seen through the scope of the New Testament. Taking the Psalms, he "studied them from the perspective of Jesus and the New Testament, and then formed them into verses for singing."[33] His studies of Psalm 98 led him to write these words:

Joy to the world! the Lord is come! Let earth receive her King;
Let ev'ry heart prepare Him room, and heav'n and nature sing.
Joy to the earth the Savior reigns. Let men their songs employ,
While fields and floods, rocks, hills and plains repeat the
sounding joy.

CHAPTER TEN - THE SONG OF REVIVAL PREACHING

No more let sins and sorrows grow, nor thorns infest the ground;
He comes to make His blessings flow far as the curse is found.
He rules the world with truth and grace, and makes the nations prove
The glories of His righteousness and wonders of His love.

Zephaniah saw the day when the King would finally be received by His creation. That did not happen on Christmas Day, but it will happen in His day.

The crescendo of glory continues as "that day" is described:

"In that day it shall be said to Jerusalem, Fear thou not: and to Zion, Let not thine hands be slack. The LORD thy God in the midst of thee is mighty; he will save, he will rejoice over thee with joy; he will rest in his love, he will joy over thee with singing" (Zephaniah 3:16-17).

The nation of Israel will be joined by saints of all tongues and nations and "fear thou not" will finally be a reality. Through its history Jerusalem has been a city besieged with fear. Righteous saints through the corridor of time have faced the enemy's sword and known the ravages of terror. But one look at Him on the throne will make dread a distant memory.

That day will be the destruction of discouragement. The phrase "let not thine hands be slack" is somewhat unfamiliar to us, but to the Hebrew man in Zephaniah's day the hand symbolized strength and power. Slack (limp) hands demonstrated a weakness and powerlessness, a hopeless discouragement that rendered a human incapable of functioning (Nehemiah 6:9).

That indescribable crowning day will not only be wonderful for us, it will be momentous for God. Our human minds allow us to imagine the moment that Jesus takes the throne, and we can paint a picture even if it is hopelessly inadequate. But on that day of salvation God will have three distinct reactions.

He will "rejoice over thee with joy." We joy in Him. We rejoice for all that He has done. We delight in His bountiful ways to us. But in this verse, we are not rejoicing, He is. He will look at Israel, the 'apple of His eye,' and will delight with a boundless joy. He will look at those He has redeemed with the love of Calvary, and rejoice. While it is easy on the human side to picture Israel rejoicing for deliverance, it is harder to imagine God experiencing such emotion, but the long struggle is over for Him as well. Like the father of Luke 15, His joy will be powerful - a joy full of joy.

He will "rest in his love." God will be speechless? He spoke the worlds into existence by His mighty word. He breathed from His mouth the words of the Bible. Yet when Jesus ascends the throne, He will simply rest in His love. He will grow quiet as He considers His endless love for Jerusalem and those that love Him. The mighty God of the Bible will have said all that needs to be said, and the picture of the throne will be worth an 'ad infinitum' of words.

Suddenly, He will "joy over thee with singing." This is the only verse in the entire Bible where God sings. Sorry

Enrique Caruso. Sorry Mario Lanza. Sorry Pavarotti. Sorry George Beverly Shea. All the human glory and rejoicing and shouting as Jesus takes the throne will suddenly turn silent as Almighty God begins to sing! His voice will ring from Heaven and we will hear a song we have never heard sung like no one has ever sung. It will be glory!

If David were here, it would be time for a 'selah'!

The preacher closes with a last great promise. "At that time will I bring you *again*, even in the time that I gather you: for I will make you a name and a praise among all people of the earth, when I turn back your captivity before your eyes, saith the LORD" (Zephaniah 3:20). The Day is coming when the tears will finally be gone, the enemy will be vanquished, and the abused will be blessed. The final captivity will be but a distant memory, as God's people are a "name and a praise" to a new world.

It will be revival beyond our imagination! A century ago, Esther Rusthoi wrote it like this:

It will be worth it all when we see Jesus,
Life's trials will seem so small when we see Christ;
One glimpse of His dear face all sorrow will erase,
So bravely run the race till we see Christ.[34]

With clouds of trouble on the political horizon and false religion abounding in the land, Zephaniah could see the answer. His eyes of faith kept him preaching when the message was offensive to the people. His confidence in the promise of God allowed him to live for another day, and his trust in the last chapter of the story meant he could preach hope in the day of despair.

And a young king was listening.

Chapter Eleven
The Long Term Results

THE QUOTABLE EVANGELIST of yesteryear, Billy Sunday, put it like this: "They tell me a revival is temporary; so is a bath, but it does you good."[35] It would not be difficult to imagine the critics in Zephaniah's day. "The revival did not last! For all of the preaching and all of the conviction and all of the reforms, what did it matter? Before long, Jerusalem was worse than ever. When Josiah was gone, the revival was gone. Look at Jehoiakim! Look at Jehoiachin! Look at Zedekiah! What's the use?"

Admittedly, many confessed works of revival have been fueled by human works creating a sensational atmosphere that produce nothing permanent. But when a revival is the product of Bible preaching, it has the promise of God that man centered programs do not have:

"So shall my word be that goeth forth out of my mouth: it shall not return unto me void, but it shall accomplish that which I please, and it shall prosper *in the thing* whereto I sent it." (Isaiah 55:11).

It may seem that the preaching of Zephaniah did not produce a lasting result, that his preaching drifted away with the desert winds of Israel, and he died without a legacy. But there were other results one might miss at first glance.

Some four miles from the bustling city of Jerusalem was the tiny village of Anathoth. We might imagine Anathoth as offering the best of both worlds. The markets of the big city were not very far away to the west, while the wilderness offered a different lifestyle to the east.

Though idols filled the land and paganism was rampant, the town was blessed with a godly priest named Hilkiah. With men of God few and far between, it is reasonable to assume he often listened to the preaching of Zephaniah. How his heart must have stirred when the sixteen year old king surrendered his life to God. What thankfulness must have filled the cottage of Hilkiah when the king took out the broom and swept away the idols. A man that loved God must have often felt as if he were the only one in the world, but the preaching of Zephaniah reminded him that others had not 'bowed unto Baal.'

Hilkiah had a son. As a boy of perhaps ten, he witnessed the boldness of Josiah in following the Lord. When he was about fourteen, he watched King Josiah demonstrate the courage of a man willing to stand alone for righteousness. A year later, that son of Hilkiah, that young man of Anathoth, received the shock of his young life:

"Then the word of the LORD came unto me, saying, Before I formed thee in the belly I knew thee; and before thou camest forth

out of the womb I sanctified thee, and I ordained thee a prophet unto the nations" (Jeremiah 1:4-5).

Fast forward thirty years. Jerusalem is teetering on the brink of the judgment of God. A lonely voice is trying to warn them of the judgment of God with these words:

"I will surely consume them, saith the LORD: there shall be no grapes on the vine, nor figs on the fig tree, and the leaf shall fade; and the things that I have given them shall pass away from them. Why do we sit still? assemble yourselves, and let us enter into the defenced cities, and let us be silent there: for the LORD our God hath put us to silence, and given us water of gall to drink, because we have sinned against the LORD" (Jeremiah 8:13-14).

One can see an old saint close his eyes and think to himself, "That's the kind of preaching we used to hear when Zephaniah was still alive!"

Hilkiah was not alone. There was another priest in the day, a man of God named Buzi. His family origins may have come from a distant eastern city, but in the days of Josiah and Zephaniah he was living in Jerusalem. At the very time when the king was removing the idols in the land the priest had a son. As the son of a priest, Buzi knew in thirty years that his boy would assume the office of the priest. How encouraged he must have been! "I grew up under Manasseh. My son is growing up under Josiah. My boy will know revival! He will be able to know and love the Word of God!"

It may be one of his son's first recollections was standing at the house of God listening to the reading of the Word of God, or perhaps sitting at the feet of Zephaniah listening to the man of God preach. Decades later, that son of a priest would be distinctly called to be a prophet of God though exiled 540 miles away in Babylon. When he preached, he might well have reminded the old-timers of Zephaniah with words like this:

"Thus saith the Lord GOD; Smite with thine hand, and stamp with thy foot, and say, Alas for all the evil abominations of the house of Israel! for they shall fall by the sword, by the famine, and by the pestilence. He that is far off shall die of the pestilence; and he that is near shall fall by the sword; and he that remaineth and is besieged shall die by the famine: thus will I accomplish my fury upon them. Then shall ye know that I am the LORD" (Ezekiel 6:11-13).

If Zephaniah held a preaching seminar, two of his possible students would be men whose names we recognize. One lifted up his voice to condemn the foreign nation of Assyria: "God *is* jealous, and the LORD revengeth; the LORD revengeth, and *is* furious; the LORD will take vengeance on his adversaries, and he reserveth *wrath* for his enemies" (Nahum 1:2). Another was a prolific writer used of God to write a message that went like this: "The mountains saw thee, *and* they trembled: the overflowing of the water passed by: the deep uttered his voice, *and* lifted up his hands on high. The sun *and* moon stood still in their habitation: at the light of thine arrows they went, *and* at the shining of thy glittering spear. Thou didst march through the land in indignation, thou didst thresh the heathen in anger" (Habakkuk 3:10-12).

I like to imagine Zephaniah preaching at a camp-like setting where the sixteen year old king decided there would be 'no turning back.' The uncompromising Bible preaching captured his convictions giving him the gumption to fight Satan and his cohorts. There was a day when Josiah "began to seek after the God of David his father" (2 Chronicles 34:3).

I wonder if years later they invited Zephaniah back to camp. The old man of God still preaches the message of surrender and dedication. He preaches to the young people that God is powerful yet merciful. He declares the 'wages of sin' warning them that the day of God's wrath is coming. Maybe his text was the story of David and Goliath, and we can almost hear him say, "God is looking for a young man who will surrender his will to Him. Where is that man that will give the Lord his body, his time, his energy, his future? Who in this crowd will say 'For to me to live *is* Christ, and to die *is* gain' (Philippians 1:21). Who will count the cost? Who will be like David and take up the cause of His name? Who will be a man of purpose?"

I can see a boy step out from the crowd. He will be the one. He will be different. He decides that following the rest of the crowd will no longer work for him, and when he comes to the end of the road, he wants to be found faithful. It will not do to set out on the path and get weary along the way. He is in it for the long haul. His life now belongs to God.

Watch him fall on his knees humbling himself before God. Look at the tears of consecration running down his cheeks. Listen to him pray: "Today I am making a choice. I choose to have a life that matters for God. I choose to be pure and undefiled. No matter what may happen in my life, I will be a man of purpose."

Little did he know that the test would come. The opportunity to sin presented itself, everyone else was doing it, but "Daniel purposed in his heart that he would not defile himself..." (Daniel 1:8).

Jeremiah. Ezekiel. Nahum. Habakkuk. Daniel. These were the product of Josiah's revival. When someone says that revival preaching does not produce permanent results, look at the index of your Bible. Ask the preachers doing a work for God where and when the Lord got their attention and they surrendered to His will. Look at the people making a difference for God, the ones living a distinct life of purpose, and almost invariably their life was changed by Zephaniah style preaching. Zephaniahs don't change with the winds of the day and they do not preach a culturally relevant message. They preach the 'Bible as it is to men as they are.' They leave the results to God and centuries of evidence prove what mighty Bible preaching produces.

So with an appropriate "saith the Lord" (Zephaniah 3:20) the man of God steps off the pages of the Word of God. I suspect he must have slept well knowing he had delivered the message of God. 2600 years later he still emboldens us to ask God for his brand of courage, to commit ourselves to preaching all the Word of God, and to forsake the popularity of the world pleasing only Him.

For when we stand in the pulpit on Sunday morning, we never really know who might be out there.

Maybe a young Josiah is out there. Or a young Jeremiah. Or a young Ezekiel. Or a young Nahum. Or a young Habakkuk. Or a young Daniel.

[1] https://www.barna.org/transformation-articles/482-voters-most-interested-in-issues-concerning-security-and-comfort-least-interested-in-moral-issues

[2] http://www.americanbible.org/state-bible

[3] Morgan, R. J. (2000). Nelson's complete book of stories, illustrations, and quotes (electronic ed., pp. 676–677). Nashville: Thomas Nelson Publishers.

[4] Galaxie Software. (2002). 10,000 Sermon Illustrations. Biblical Studies Press.

[5] Galaxie Software. (2002). 10,000 Sermon Illustrations. Biblical Studies Press.

[6] Elwell, W. A., & Beitzel, B. J. (1988).Baker encyclopedia of the Bible. Grand Rapids, MI: Baker Book House.

[7] Morgan, R. J. (2000). Nelson's complete book of stories, illustrations, and quotes (electronic ed., pp. 303–304). Nashville: Thomas Nelson Publishers.

[8] Patterson, R. D. (2003). Nahum, Habakkuk, Zephaniah. Minor Prophets Exegetical Commentary (p. 268). Biblical Studies Press.

[9] English Stand Version (ESV); Revised Standard Version (RSV); New International Version (NIV); The text of the New American Standard Version (NASV) says "remove away."

[10] Barker, K. L. (1999). Vol. 20: Micah, Nahum, Habakkuk, Zephaniah. The New American Commentary (430). Nashville: Broadman & Holman Publishers.

[11] Boice, J. M. (2002). The Minor Prophets: an expositional commentary (p. 442). Grand Rapids, MI: Baker Books.

[12] Barker, K. L. (1999). Vol. 20: Micah, Nahum, Habakkuk, Zephaniah. The New American Commentary (434). Nashville: Broadman & Holman Publishers.

[13]   Adams, Moody (1997). The Titanic's Last Hero. West Columbia, SC: The Olive Press

[14] http://www.brainyquote.com/quotes/authors/b/bill_cosby.html

[15]   http://cnsnews.com/news/article/1183700-violent-crimes-committed-public-schools-only-303900-reported-police

[16]   Sorenson, David H. (2006). Understanding the Bible (An Independent Baptist Commentary). Duluth: Northstar Ministries.

[17]   Robertson, O. Palmer. (1990). The Books of Nahum, Habakkuk, & Zephaniah. New International Commentary on the Old Testament. Grand Rapids: Wm. B. Eerdmans Publishing Co.

[18] Patterson, R. D. (2003). Nahum, Habakkuk, Zephaniah. Minor Prophets Exegetical Commentary (p. 288). Biblical Studies Press.

[19] Ibid.

[20]   Rusten, S. with E. Michael. (2005). The Complete Book of When & Where in the Bible and Throughout History. Wheaton, IL: Tyndale House Publishers, Inc.

[21]   Anon, 2000. AMG Bible Illustrations, Chattanooga: AMG Publishers.

[22]   http://www.sonofthesouth.net/slavery/abraham-lincoln/abraham-lincoln-richmond.htm

[23] https://www.youtube.com/embed/OvN1jTkzXbY?rel=0

[24]   Boice, J. M. (2002). The Minor Prophets: an expositional commentary (p. 445). Grand Rapids, MI: Baker Books.

[25]   Boice, J. M. (2002). The Minor Prophets: an expositional commentary (pp. 450–451). Grand Rapids, MI: Baker Books.

[26]   Robertson, O. Palmer. (1990). The Books of Nahum, Habakkuk, & Zephaniah. New International Commentary on the Old Testament. Grand Rapids: Wm. B. Eerdmans Publishing Co.

[27] A tremendous collection of Richard Anderson's preaching is available at:
http://kjvgalatians220.com

[28] http://www.jesus-is-savior.com/Wolves/robert_schuller.htm

[29] http://articles.latimes.com/1990-05-04/news/vw-404_1_ted-turner

[30] Hobbs, H. H. (1990). My favorite illustrations. Nashville, TN: Broadman Press.

[31] Let's Have A Revival. Joel Hemphill.

[32] AMG Bible Illustrations. (2000). Chattanooga: AMG Publishers.

[33] Morgan, Robert J. (2004). Then Sings My Soul - Book Two (p. 24). Nashville, TN: Thomas Nelson.

[34] When We See Christ. Esther Kerr Rusthoi.

[35] Morgan, R. J. (2000). Nelson's complete book of stories, illustrations, and quotes (electronic ed., p. 672). Nashville: Thomas Nelson Publishers.

Books By Paul Schwanke

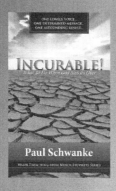

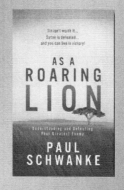

Evangelist Paul Schwanke
www.preachthebible.com

14782848R00055

Made in the USA
San Bernardino, CA
04 September 2014